WHAT'S THE SMALLEST
THING YOU CAN THINK OF?

A flea? A crumb? A grain of sand or a speck of dust? Well, from my point of view, all these things are MASSIVE!

I'm a tiny particle called a quark, but you can call me Q.

For Chrissie, the real scientist —CE

To Linda Clark, a great artist, a dear friend, and an inspiring teacher —PD

QUANTUM!

THE STRANGE SCIENCE OF THE
SMALLEST STUFF IN THE UNIVERSE

CHRISTOPHER EDGE

illustrated by
PAUL DAVIZ

CANDLEWICK PRESS

WELCOME TO THE QUANTUM UNIVERSE

Every living thing and object in the universe, from the biggest star to the smallest speck of dust, is made of atoms. EVEN YOU!

You can't see an atom—not without a very, VERY powerful microscope to help you—because it's just too small. For a long time, scientists thought that atoms were the tiniest things in existence. But inside atoms are even smaller particles called protons, neutrons, and electrons. And inside a proton or a neutron, you'll find me—a quark!

To give you an idea of how incredibly tiny an atom is, a single grain of sand, depending on its size, can contain 43 quintillion atoms. That's 43,000,000,000,000,000,000 atoms!

A quark is an ELEMENTARY PARTICLE, which means it can't be divided into smaller particles. Some elementary particles, including quarks like me, are MATTER PARTICLES, the building blocks that make the stuff that fills the universe. Other elementary particles are FORCE PARTICLES like photons and gluons.

BEING TINY IS FUN

If you could behave like a particle, you'd be able to read this book *and* play a video game at the same time in different rooms of your house, teleport from one place to another, and even walk through a solid wall!

It might sound like science fiction, but the weird way that my friends and I behave powers the universe. It's the reason why the sun shines and a smartphone works.

Scientists are very interested in subatomic particles (particles smaller than an atom) like me and call the rules that we follow quantum physics.

In this book I'm going to take you on a mind-blowing tour. We'll travel from the Big Bang to the heart of a black hole and have a race inside the biggest machine that's ever been built. We'll make a pit stop in a parallel world, and you'll even find out how a cat could be dead and alive at the same time . . .

So let's take a ride into the QUANTUM UNIVERSE!

THE BIG BANG

We'll start our tour 13.8 billion years ago, at the moment the universe began.

The universe is EVERYTHING that exists, and it is VERY BIG. It contains hundreds of billions of galaxies, trillions of stars, and countless planets, including ours—the planet Earth. But scientists think the universe started out as a tiny speck, much smaller than me, and *incredibly* hot.

The Big Bang was when this tiny universe got very big very fast. In less than a millionth of a second, the universe grew to about the size of our solar system!

THE SUN

**27,000,000
degrees Fahrenheit
(15,000,000 degrees Celsius)
at the sun's core**

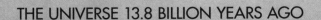

THE UNIVERSE 13.8 BILLION YEARS AGO

18,000,000,000 degrees Fahrenheit (10,000,000,000 degrees Celsius)
That's a lot of zeros!

COOL DOWN

As the universe continued to get bigger, it started to cool down too. The super-fast quarks slowed down just enough to be captured by the strong nuclear force. This force is carried by another particle called the gluon.

Gluons stick quarks together to create brand-new particles called protons and neutrons.

Along with electrons, these are the building blocks that make atoms—which can then make ALL the stuff in the universe. And all this started in a split second.

Phew!

WATCH OUT!

This early universe was like a giant bowl of subatomic soup. Fizzing with energy, pairs of particles kept popping into existence: quarks and our evil twins, antiquarks!

Whenever a quark and an antiquark meet, there's trouble. Both particles are destroyed and release lots of energy.

Zooming around at high speed, quarks and antiquarks kept bumping into each other. If the number of quarks and antiquarks had been equal, they would all have been destroyed, and the universe would now be completely empty. There would be nobody reading this book! So scientists think there must have been more quarks than antiquarks in the early universe. We won!

A PROTON is made of two UP quarks and one DOWN quark.

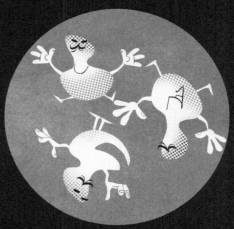

A NEUTRON is made of one UP quark and two DOWN quarks.

INSIDE THE ATOM

Everything in the universe is made out of atoms, but how exactly is an atom made?
Well, you need three special types of particles and a little bit of force!

The subatomic particles you need to build an atom are called protons, neutrons, and electrons.
HI, GUYS!

MEASURING THE QUANTUM WORLD

If someone asks how tall you are, you can tell them your height in feet and inches. But these units and even centimeters and millimeters are all TOO BIG to measure super-small things like atoms and particles. We're going to need a tinier ruler . . .

LET'S GET NANO

A NANOMETER is a MILLION times smaller than a millimeter. We use nanometers to measure things like viruses, transistors on computer chips, and other teeny-tiny stuff we can only see under a microscope.

THE ABSOLUTELY TINY

A PICOMETER is a BILLION times smaller than a millimeter. A molecule of water is made of two hydrogen atoms (H_2) stuck to one oxygen atom (O). This is what gives water its scientific name: H_2O. And one single molecule of water measures 275 picometers across.

SPARKS WILL FLY

Protons have a positive charge, while electrons have a negative charge. (The neutral neutrons don't have any charge.) Something called the electromagnetic force makes opposite charges attract, and it's this force that holds the atom together. It keeps the electrons whizzing around the protons—almost as if they're trying to impress them!

Protons and neutrons are in the center of the atom, which is called the nucleus. Protons and neutrons are held together here by the strong nuclear force, which sticks them together like superglue. Electrons can be found whizzing around the nucleus, and they exist in different layers around it, called shells. Each shell can fit only up to a certain number of electrons, and when it's full, a new shell is started. The very first atoms made were the simplest ones: HYDROGEN and HELIUM.

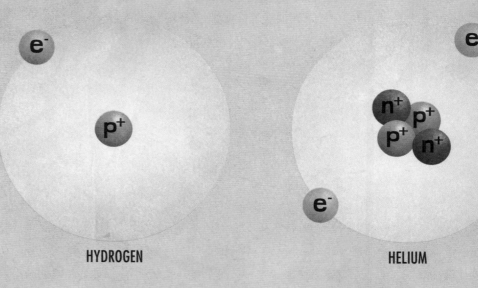

HYDROGEN

HELIUM

ITSY-BITSY TEENY-WEENY SUBATOMIC SCALES

A FEMTOMETER is a TRILLION times smaller than 1 millimeter. A proton is a little less than 1 femtometer wide, and so is a neutron—a neutron is just a little bit bigger than a proton. But electrons are EVEN SMALLER—they're so small that scientists treat them like tiny dots with no size at all.

DO THE PLANCK

There's also something called PLANCK TIME, which is the smallest possible unit of time. One second consists of about 100,000,000,000,000,000,000, 000,000,000,000,000,000, 000,000 of these units!

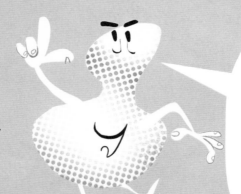

Psst! The really big surprise when you look inside an atom is what isn't there. Most of an atom is made up of empty space! Atoms, which make up everything that exists, are mostly made of NOTHING!

HOW TO BUILD A STAR

A star is a giant ball of gas that produces light and heat.
In the sky on a sunny day you'll see our planet's closest star—the sun!

At night, you might be able to see thousands of stars. But for the first hundred million years after the Big Bang, there was no light and the only atoms that existed were hydrogen and helium. The universe was still expanding, but it took another force of nature to really make it shine!

GRAVITY is a force that pulls things together—
from the tiniest atoms to supermassive stars! The more
mass a thing has, the greater its gravitational pull.
Mass is the amount of matter, or stuff, a thing has in it.
To find out the mass of an atom, you just add
up its protons and neutrons.

TURN ON THE LIGHTS

In the early universe, like now, there were lots more hydrogen atoms than helium atoms, and they were spread more thickly in some places. In these lumpy parts, the mass was greater than where the atoms were more evenly spread out. The force of gravity pulled more atoms into each lump, turning them into big clumps, then into huge swirling clouds of gas.

And inside these clouds, something very interesting started to happen . . .

The birth of a star happens when gravity pulls clumps of hydrogen atoms more tightly together until they fuse into helium.

As gravity packed the atoms together at the core, the clouds of gas that got big enough began to turn into stars! The temperature kept rising as the atoms were squeezed even more, becoming hotter than our own sun. In this incredible heat, hydrogen nuclei fused together to form helium nuclei. This generated huge amounts of energy in the form of heat and light.

Scientists call this NUCLEAR FUSION. It powers every star and makes them all shine!

Psst! If you have more than one nucleus, you call them nuclei!

A SUPERNOVA OF STUFF

From planets and stars to skyscrapers and sharks, the universe is full of *stuff*!

All this stuff is made out of atoms, arranged into three different forms: SOLIDS, LIQUIDS, and GASES. What type of solid, liquid, or gas you get depends on the atoms inside it. To find out what type of atom you've got, you need to count its protons. An atom of hydrogen has only one proton, while an atom of lead has eighty-two protons. HEAVY METAL!

Let's start with the hard stuff— SOLIDS! In a solid, all the atoms are neatly arranged, lock tightly together, and always stay in the same position. This is what gives a solid like this iron block its shape. Ouch!

Next we get the wet stuff—LIQUIDS! In a liquid, the atoms aren't touching as closely as in a solid, which lets the atoms slide over one another. This slippery ability is what lets you pour a nice refreshing drink. Cheers!

Finally there are GASES—some of which make up the air you're breathing right now! Inside this helium balloon, the atoms of gas are spread farther apart and fizz around at fast speeds, touching briefly only when they bump into each other. Excuse me!

ELEMENTARY

When a substance can't be broken down into any other substance, we call that an ELEMENT. Almost every element around you—hydrogen, lead, or the oxygen you breathe—was made by a star. In the super-hot, super-dense center of a star—the core—atoms are squeezed together so tightly that they fuse to create brand-new elements!

MAKE WAY FOR THE NEW

For most of their lives, stars fuse hydrogen atoms together to make brand-new helium atoms. But in the most massive stars, after all the hydrogen atoms are used up, helium atoms start fusing together to create other elements—carbon, oxygen, and more! A star's core gets smaller and hotter as heavier and heavier elements are made . . . until finally it turns into iron.

Sometimes, in a star's last second of life, the atoms inside its core are condensed so tightly that the star explodes, flinging all the elements it's already made across the universe and creating new ones too, like silver and gold. This super-hot, SUPER-HUGE explosion is called a supernova.

LET THERE BE LIGHT!

I want to introduce you to a friend of mine who really brightens my day. Meet the PHOTON!

The photon is an elementary particle of light, but it can also act like a wave. Sounds confusing, right? Well, let's shed a little light on the situation!

THE ELECTROMAGNETIC SPECTRUM

The light we see with our eyes is called VISIBLE LIGHT, but this is only one type of electromagnetic radiation.

RADIO WAVES have the longest wavelengths and carry TV signals as well as the songs you hear on the radio. A single radio wave can be larger than our planet!

MICROWAVES can heat up your dinner, but they're also used for communication. From mobile phone calls to satellite broadcasts, microwave radiation helps us keep in touch.

INFRARED radiation transmits heat. You can't see it with your eyes, but you feel it on your skin when you stand outside on a sunny day. It's also what makes your TV remote work!

ELECTROMAGNETIC RADIATION

Light is a form of energy called ELECTROMAGNETIC RADIATION. It travels in waves. And just like waves in the sea, these electromagnetic waves can be measured in two different ways.

WAVELENGTH is the distance from the peak of one wave to the peak of the next.

FREQUENCY is the number of waves that pass by a certain point in a set period of time.

Long waves have a low frequency, while short waves have a high frequency. The higher the frequency, the higher the energy.

The green wave above has twice the frequency of the red one, but it has half the wavelength.

VISIBLE LIGHT is in the middle of the electromagnetic spectrum and is made of a rainbow of colors: red, orange, yellow, green, blue, indigo, and violet. Each color has a different wavelength.

ULTRAVIOLET rays can kill harmful bacteria but can also give you sunburn. Some animals, like butterflies, can see ultraviolet light.

X-RAYS are high-energy waves of radiation that can pass through solid objects—including the human body! Doctors use X-rays to take photos of broken bones, while astronomers look for X-rays in space when searching for black holes.

GAMMA RAYS have a very short wavelength and a high frequency. These high-energy waves can be used to treat diseases like cancer.

LIGHT-YEARS AND TIME TRAVEL

In the emptiness of space, a photon of light travels at a constant 186,282 miles (299,792 kilometers) per second. That's 671 million miles (1.07 billion kilometers) per hour!

If you could travel as fast as a photon, you would be moving at the speed of light and could make it around the world seven times in less than a second! But because you have mass, you would never be able to travel at the speed of light. As you go faster and faster, the energy needed to move you would become greater and greater and eventually infinite.

LIGHT-YEARS are used by astronomers to measure the HUGE distances there are in the universe. A light-year is how far a photon can travel in a year. The closest star to our sun is Proxima Centauri, which is a whopping 25,300,000,000,000 miles (40,208,000,000,000 kilometers) away. It takes photons of light from this star 4.25 years to reach us here on Earth, so we say the distance to Proxima Centauri is 4.25 light-years.

OUR GALAXY, the Milky Way, is about 100,000 light-years across, while astronomers reckon the universe—well, all the parts of it we can see—is an incredible 93 billion light-years wide!

PHOTONS CAN LIVE FOREVER. From the moment a photon is born, it keeps traveling at the speed of light until it reaches an object and gets absorbed. When you look up at the stars in the night sky, the photons of light that you see might have been traveling for millions of years until the moment they hit your eye.

PHOTONS REVEAL THE PAST! Whenever a photon hits your eye, it brings you information about the place it came from. This is how you see the world around you. When you look at the stars, you are seeing them at the very moment the photons set out on their journey, maybe millions of years ago. This means photons let you see into the past!

19

GIANTS, DWARFS, AND SOME SERIOUSLY HEAVY STARS

There could be more than 10,000 TRILLION stars in the universe! Just like you humans, stars come in different sizes—from supergiants to strange stars a fraction of the size. Have you ever wondered what happens when a star runs out of fuel? It all depends on how MASSIVE the star is . . .

RED GIANTS

Stars the mass of our sun grow to become RED GIANTS. In a red giant, all the hydrogen atoms inside the core have been used up, so the hydrogen atoms in the outer layers start fusing into helium too. This makes the star grow bigger and brighter.

If this dot

.

represents the size of our sun right now, this balloon is how big it will become! When our sun turns into a red giant billions of years from now, it will swallow Mercury, Venus, and maybe even Earth!

WHITE DWARFS

A red giant can't live forever. Its outer layers slowly drift off into space, leaving behind a core that might be smaller than planet Earth. This is all that's left of the star and is called a WHITE DWARF.

NEUTRON STARS

Stars that are even bigger than red giants are called SUPERGIANTS. Instead of becoming a white dwarf, a supergiant explodes in a supernova and can leave behind a NEUTRON STAR. This strange spinning sphere is about the size of a city, often measuring only 12.5 miles (20 kilometers) across. Don't let its size fool you, though. This neutron star is still HEAVIER than our sun. But all its mass has been squeezed into such a small space that it's now super dense!

Just one tablespoon of stuff from the core of a neutron star would weigh the same as Mount Everest!

PULSARS

Some neutron stars spit out energetic beams of radiation from their north and south magnetic poles. Astronomers can spot these beams only when they're pointing directly at Earth, and because the neutron star is spinning so fast, the beams look like flashing pulses of radiation. It's a bit like watching a lighthouse that is stuck on fast-forward! This kind of neutron star is called a PULSAR.

Psst! One of the fastest pulsars ever detected rotates around 40,000 times in a minute, so a day on this star lasts for much less than a second!

BLACK HOLES

It's time to take a trip to one of the strangest places in the universe.

A black hole is what is left behind after one of the very biggest stars in the universe explodes. Gravity is so strong here that not even light can escape, making black holes invisible. Astronomers think that there is a supermassive black hole at the center of every galaxy. The black hole in the center of our galaxy is called Sagittarius A*. Don't worry—it's more than 25,000 light-years away!

POINT OF NO RETURN

Around every black hole is an invisible border called the EVENT HORIZON. Across this invisible line, the black hole's gravitational pull becomes so strong that nothing, not even light, can escape.

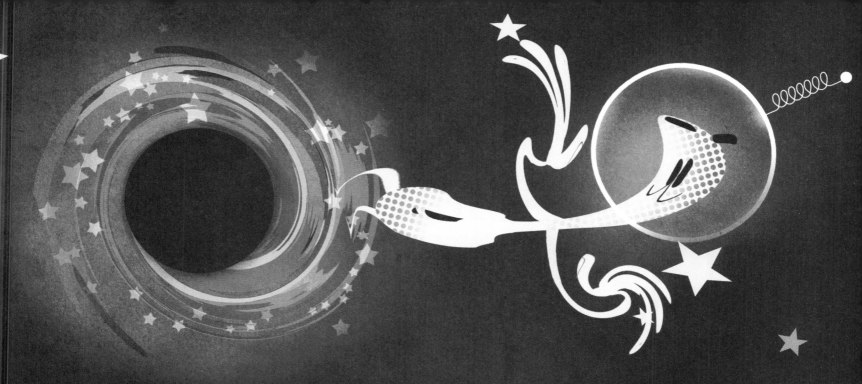

STRRRRRRRRRRRETCH . . .

If you were unlucky enough to fall feetfirst into a black hole, the gravitational pull on your toes would be stronger than the gravitational pull on your head. This difference in gravity would start to pull you apart, stretching out all the atoms in your body like a long strand of spaghetti! This is called spaghettification, and it happens to everything that falls inside a black hole.

NO-MAN'S-LAND

The strangest part of a black hole is found at its center. We don't really know what goes on in a black hole because we can't see inside. The math formulas that make up the rules of the universe no longer make sense inside a black hole either. Some scientists call this point the SINGULARITY, while other scientists hypothesize that you'll find a WORMHOLE there instead—a tunnel that could connect the black hole to a brand-new universe. Maybe you will figure it out someday!

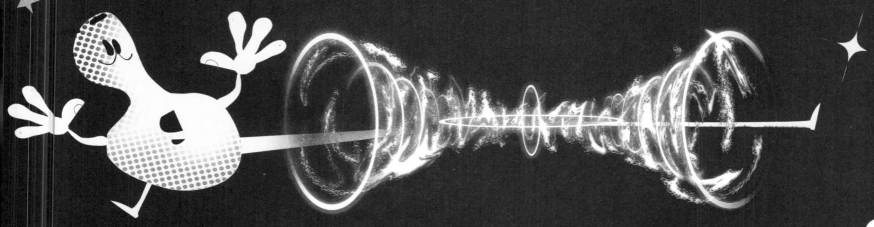

THIS BANANA IS RADIOACTIVE!

Most things in the world are a little bit radioactive—even this BANANA!

It contains radioactive potassium atoms. But don't throw your fruit bowl out the window!
The amount of radiation emitted by a banana is microscopically tiny. You'd have to eat around
50 MILLION bananas for the radiation to harm you—and only if you ate them all at once!
In fact, your body contains more potassium than a banana.

Which means that YOU ARE RADIOACTIVE!

HOW DOES RADIOACTIVITY WORK?

At the center of every atom is a nucleus. This is made out of protons and, in most types of atoms, some neutrons too. In an unstable atom, these particles break away from the nucleus, and this means the atom is RADIOACTIVE!

The particles are released in the form of RADIATION. There are different types of radiation, depending on the type of particle that's kicked out and the energy that is emitted.

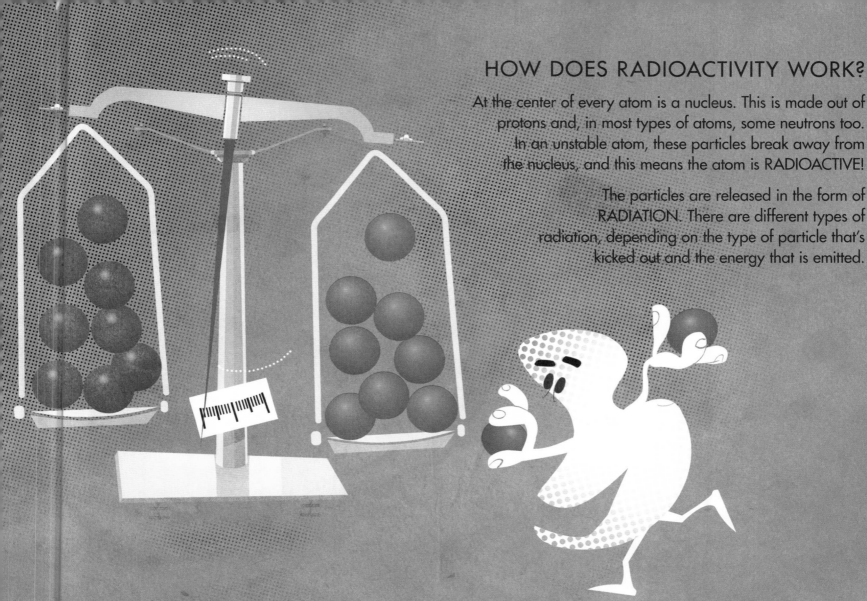

ALPHA RADIATION (α) is made of alpha particles. An alpha particle is a cluster of two protons and two neutrons stuck together (a.k.a. a helium nucleus).

BETA RADIATION (β) is made of beta particles. A beta particle is an electron or a positron (a positive electron). These high-energy particles shoot out of the atom whenever an extra neutron in the nucleus turns into a proton or an extra proton turns into a neutron.

GAMMA RADIATION (γ) is made of photons with a high frequency that are known as gamma rays. The atom releases these photons to get rid of the energy produced by changes in the nucleus.

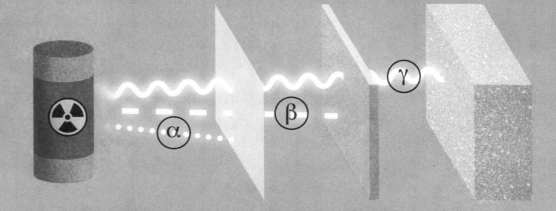

Alpha particles can be stopped by a sheet of paper. Beta particles can be stopped by an aluminum plate. Gamma radiation can be stopped by a few feet (about a meter) of concrete.

25

$E = mc^2$

$E = mc^2$ is probably the most famous equation in science. It was first explained in 1905 by scientist Albert Einstein and it changed the world. But what exactly does it mean?

E is ENERGY.

c is the SPEED OF LIGHT, and the little number ^{2} means you multiply the value in front of it by itself.

m is MASS—the amount of matter a thing has in it.

The equation tells us that MATTER can be turned into ENERGY (and energy can be turned into matter). In fact, the TINIEST atom holds potentially MASSIVE amounts of energy.

But you need to SPLIT THE ATOM to make this transformation.

TIME TO SPLIT

NUCLEAR REACTIONS happen in the center of an atom—its NUCLEUS. Protons and neutrons are held together in the nucleus by the strong nuclear force. Splitting the atom's nucleus releases this energy. This is called NUCLEAR FISSION. You can split atoms of any element, but the easiest ones to split are those with the largest nuclei, such as uranium. Nuclear fission leaves behind dangerous radioactive waste. So don't try splitting atoms at home!

LET'S SPLIT THIS URANIUM ATOM!

First, we fire a neutron at a nucleus of uranium-235, which is made up of 92 protons and 143 neutrons.

If the neutron hits the nucleus at just the right speed, it is absorbed, and then the nucleus splits into two. This releases the energy that was locked up inside the nucleus.

When the nucleus splits apart, stray neutrons are also set free. If one of these neutrons hits another nucleus, it will split it in two as well! This can keep happening and cause a CHAIN REACTION! In just a split second, MASSIVE amounts of energy are emitted.

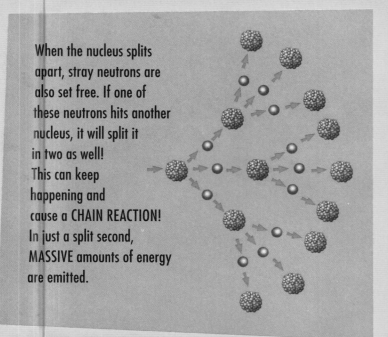

LET'S CONNECT

The other type of nuclear reaction is NUCLEAR FUSION. This is the opposite of nuclear fission. Instead of splitting an atom apart, nuclear fusion joins two atomic nuclei together to make a brand-new atom. This releases EVEN MORE energy than nuclear fission!

HOW TO SPOT A PARTICLE

Ever wished you could be in more than one place at the same time? Maybe you'd still like to be tucked in bed at the same time as you're waiting in the rain for the school bus. Well, in the quantum world, some particles seem to be in more than one place at the same time!

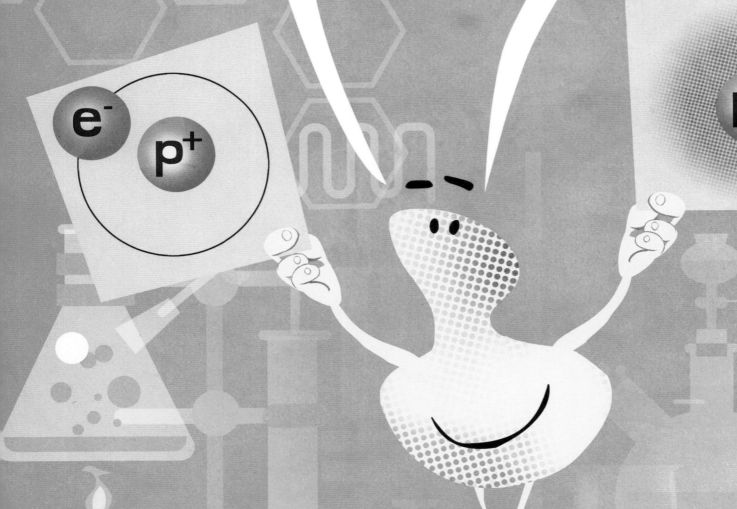

It can be tricky to tell exactly where an electron is. We often draw pictures to represent electrons, like this one showing a hydrogen atom with one electron whizzing around a nucleus made of a single proton.

However, the electron is actually spread out in a cloud around the nucleus. This is a cloud of possibilities that shows you ALL the possible places the electron could be!

HIDE-AND-PEEK

Some scientists think it's only when you start looking for the electron that it decides where it is going to be.

I'm going to fire a single electron at a screen, which will light up in the exact place where the electron hits it. But I've put the screen in a box to keep anyone from peeking in. We can see the place where the particle has been fired into the box . . .

and we can see where it hit the screen. But which way did it go to get there?

The electron behaved like a wave spreading out across the space of the box. It's only when you try to detect it—using the screen—that the electron remembers to act like a particle again.

Just taking a look causes the wave of possibilities to collapse into one possibility. And that's the place you find the electron.

So an electron can possibly be in LOTS of different places simultaneously. But only when you're NOT looking. And this is true for EVERY particle in the quantum universe.

ZOMBIE CATS AND PARALLEL WORLDS

How can a particle know when you're watching it? The physicist Erwin Schrödinger thought this was too strange to be true and invented an experiment to prove it. Prepare to meet SCHRÖDINGER'S CAT!

Inside this sealed box is: a bottle of poison, a hammer, a Geiger counter (which measures radiation), a lump of uranium, and . . . a cat.

Every second, there's a 50 percent chance that the uranium will spit out a radioactive particle. If this happens, the Geiger counter will detect the radiation and trigger the hammer, making it fall and smash open the bottle of poison. And if this happens, the cat will DIE!

Psst! Don't worry— no real cats were harmed in the cause of quantum physics. This was an imaginary experiment!

A ZOMBIE-CAT-MAKING MACHINE

But particles can be in more than one state at the same time, and it's only when you OBSERVE the particle that its state becomes fixed. Before then, the radioactive particle will be in both possible states—DECAYED and UNDECAYED— simultaneously! This means the Geiger counter HAS and HASN'T detected any radiation. The hammer HAS and HASN'T fallen. The bottle of poison HAS and HASN'T smashed. All these different possibilities exist simultaneously. Until you open the lid of the box and take a look inside, the cat is DEAD and ALIVE at the same time!

A PARALLEL UNIVERSE?

Some scientists think that when you take a look at a particle to see what place or state it's in, all the other possible places or states it could be in don't just disappear—they actually all exist in PARALLEL UNIVERSES!

Each universe is real, but we only SEE the outcome that happened in the universe we live in.

The idea that the universe we live in is constantly splitting into new parallel universes is called the MANY-WORLDS INTERPRETATION. There could be a parallel universe where the dinosaurs never became extinct and a universe where you've just become the first person to set foot on Mars!

Some scientists think there might be an INFINITE number of parallel universes and they call this the MULTIVERSE.

Neutrinos weigh almost NOTHING, and they don't like to interact with ordinary matter like the atoms that you're made of. In fact, most neutrinos zip right through planet Earth as if it wasn't even there! But scientists have come up with some clever ways to detect them.

GHOST PARTICLES

While you are reading these words, billions of subatomic particles are passing through your body and you don't even notice them!

These ghostly particles are called NEUTRINOS and they have been around since less than a second after the Big Bang. They are made all the time: in the core of the Sun, in nuclear reactors, even inside a banana! From nuclear fusion to radioactive decay, neutrinos can be created in lots of different ways. And this means there are LOTS of them around.

A GIANT SWIMMING POOL INSIDE A TIN CAN

The SUPER-K neutrino detector is built under a mountain in Japan, more than half a mile (a thousand meters) underground. The detector is made out of a huge stainless steel tank, which is filled with 55,100 tons (50,000 metric tons) of water. As we know, water is H_2O—two atoms of hydrogen stuck to one atom of oxygen. The detector helps scientists see if any of these atoms are hit by a stray neutrino. If this happens, there is a flash of light that is captured by one of the thirteen thousand light detectors lining the inside of the tank. Using these detectors, scientists can track the path of the neutrino to see where it has come from. This could be the sun, a distant star, or even a supermassive black hole!

The light detectors inside are made of gold-tipped tubes, which really make the Super-K shine!

WHAT'S YOUR FLAVOR?

Neutrinos come in different types, like ice-cream flavors. There are electron neutrinos, muon neutrinos, and tau neutrinos, but the strange thing is that a neutrino can CHANGE its flavor too. Imagine eating ice cream and finding that it changes from vanilla to chocolate before turning into strawberry. Well, that's what a neutrino can do as it travels almost at the speed of light!

SUPER COLD, SUPER STRANGE!

Imagine things that start to float in midair and liquids that climb up the sides of walls!
When stuff gets super cold, it can behave in SUPER-STRANGE ways.
The lowest possible temperature is called ABSOLUTE ZERO. To give you an idea of how incredibly cold this is, the freezing point of water is 32 degrees Fahrenheit (0 degrees Celsius), but absolute zero is a frosty minus 459.67 degrees Fahrenheit (minus 273.15 degrees Celsius).

THE KELVIN SCALE

Scientists use a different temperature scale to measure things that get super cold. This is called the KELVIN SCALE, after Lord Kelvin, the scientist who worked it out. Absolute zero is 0 K—that's zero K, not OK! At this temperature, atoms have no heat energy. It's impossible to get THAT cold, but when you get close, strange physical effects can be seen. One of these effects is the MEISSNER EFFECT. This weird phenomenon can let you levitate a magnet in midair!

Water boils: 373.15 K

Hottest land temperature recorded on Earth—Death Valley, USA: 329.85 K

Water freezes: 273.15 K

Coldest temperature recorded on Earth—Vostok Station, Antarctica: 183.95 K

Absolute zero: 0 K

LET'S GET LEVITATING

When the temperature gets cold enough, some metals turn into SUPERCONDUCTORS. This means they LOVE electricity but HATE magnetism. If you try to place a magnet over a SUPERCONDUCTOR, it will push the magnet away. And this can make the magnet float in midair! Scientists call this MAGNETIC LEVITATION.

SUPERFLUIDS

Most liquids are frozen solid by the time the temperature reads absolute zero, but LIQUID HELIUM turns into a SUPERFLUID. In a superfluid, all the atoms behave in exactly the same way. There are no bumps or collisions between them, which means a superfluid can flow up a straw on its own, climb the walls of any container you put it into, and even start leaking out the bottom of a container if it finds any microscopic cracks. If you give a superfluid a stir, the liquid will keep spinning forever!

35

YOUR QUANTUM WORLD

You might think that because you're so BIG, quantum physics doesn't matter to you.

After all, it just describes the ways that teeny-tiny particles behave, right?
Well, LOTS OF THINGS that you use EVERY DAY exist only because of QUANTUM PHYSICS!
From smartphones to computers to shopping, we need and use quantum physics constantly.

MORE CHIPS, PLEASE

Smartphones, computers, and electronic devices contain chips that are about the size of your fingernail, and each of these microchips contains BILLIONS of transistors. A transistor is basically an incredibly tiny gate designed to let electrons through. When the gate is open, electrons charge through it, and when it's closed, they can't. When transistors work together, they help computers make the BITS—the zeros and ones—that allow your device to work. Transistors open and close up to FOUR BILLION times every second and sometimes even faster!

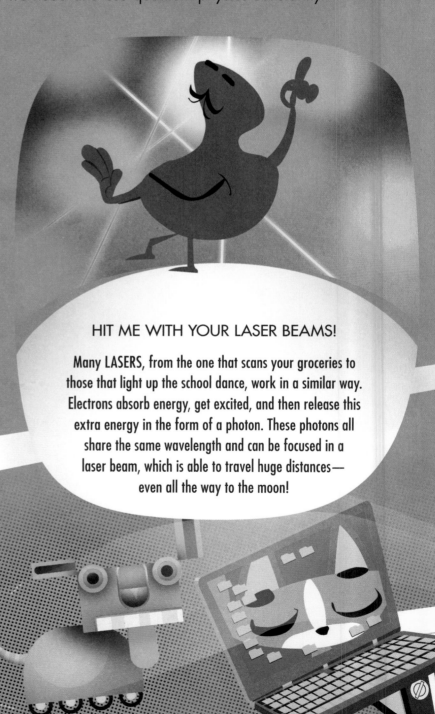

HIT ME WITH YOUR LASER BEAMS!

Many LASERS, from the one that scans your groceries to those that light up the school dance, work in a similar way. Electrons absorb energy, get excited, and then release this extra energy in the form of a photon. These photons all share the same wavelength and can be focused in a laser beam, which is able to travel huge distances— even all the way to the moon!

DOCTOR QUANTUM

Doctors use quantum physics all the time to help make people better. From X-rays that can spot broken bones to gamma rays that can be used to treat certain diseases, the photon is the doctor's friendly helper! A machine called an MRI scanner uses radio frequencies and magnets to spin the protons in a patient's body, giving a picture of what it looks like inside as the protons spin back into position. This scanner can even let a doctor look inside a patient's brain!

SMALL BUT MIGHTY

Scientists have used the strange phenomenon of quantum tunneling to build the MOST POWERFUL microscope in the world. This is called a SCANNING TUNNELING MICROSCOPE, and it can show things SO SMALL that you can even see what an atom looks like!

SCIENCE FACT OR SCIENCE FICTION?

Would you like to be able to teleport anywhere or walk through a wall like a ghost?

QUANTUM TUNNELING

If you were silly enough to try walking through a solid wall, you'd end up with a very sore nose! However, that's not necessarily the case in the quantum universe. When a particle hits a barrier, the particle can behave like a wave. With a small barrier—less than a nanometer thick—a tiny ripple can leak through to the other side, giving you a very small chance of finding the particle there. And sometimes, you do! This strange phenomenon is called QUANTUM TUNNELING.

BEAM ME UP?

Can particles teleport? Well, not exactly. But different particles can exchange information in a connection called QUANTUM TELEPORTATION. It begins with QUANTUM ENTANGLEMENT, where the QUANTUM STATES of different particles are connected. The quantum state of a particle describes EVERYTHING about it.

When two particles are entangled, a MEASUREMENT made of one particle changes it AND the other particle at the same time. And what the second particle is doing is the opposite of the first! This is true even if the entangled particles are BILLIONS OF MILES apart. So if you find that one of the particles is spinning one way, this means that its twin must be spinning the other way! This spooky connection makes the exchange of information between different particles possible.

FUTURE INVENTIONS

NANOTECHNOLOGY is about using atoms and molecules to invent super-cool stuff.

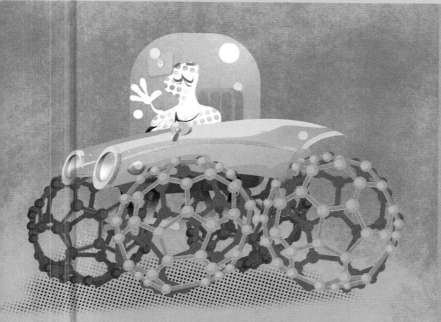

NANOCARS

These molecule-sized motors have wheels made of BUCKYBALLS, which are football-shaped spheres made out of sixty carbon atoms. Scientists hope that one day these nanocars, which are small enough to move through your bloodstream, will help transform medicine.

INVISIBILITY CLOAKS

If you want to make yourself INVISIBLE, nanotechnology might be able to help! Scientists can now change the way atoms are arranged in a material, giving these METAMATERIALS special new powers. The photons of light bouncing off this page and hitting your eyes let you SEE this book. But in a metamaterial, the atoms can be structured in a way that makes photons of light flow over and around it. This makes the metamaterial INVISIBLE! So far this is possible only for low wavelengths of light, like RADIO WAVES, but maybe someday you'll be able to wear a real-life cloak of invisibility!

QUANTUM COMPUTERS

The superfast QUANTUM COMPUTER is no ordinary computer. Ordinary computers use bits—ZEROS and ONES—but a quantum computer uses QUBITS! A qubit is both zero AND one at the same time, and a qubit can do LOTS of complex calculations at once. But a quantum computer must be kept VERY cold—colder than outer space!

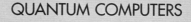

IT'S TIME TO MEET THE FAMILY!

You can get UP QUARKS and DOWN QUARKS, TOP QUARKS and BOTTOM QUARKS—even
STRANGE QUARKS and CHARM QUARKS. And these quarks come in different "colors": red, green, and blue.

These colors are the names scientists give to the STRONG FORCE charge that each quark carries.
The strong force is what helps GLUONS glue quarks into larger particles, like protons and neutrons.
Different "colored" quarks attract each other, so inside every proton you'll find a red, blue, and green quark.

UP QUARK

TOP QUARK

STRANGE QUARK

DOWN QUARK

BOTTOM QUARK

CHARM QUARK

INSIDE THE LARGE HADRON COLLIDER

If you want to simulate what the universe was like just after the Big Bang,
then you need to build a PARTICLE ACCELERATOR!

A particle accelerator is a MASSIVE machine that's used to smash atoms together. Let's take a ride around the BIGGEST and MOST POWERFUL particle accelerator in the world—the LARGE HADRON COLLIDER. It's buried deep underground and shaped like a giant racetrack. You won't find cars racing through this 17-mile (27-kilometer) tunnel; instead, tiny beams of protons are fired in opposite directions and whizz around and around, getting faster and faster until they're traveling almost at the speed of light. And then they crash into each other!

When protons smash together at such high speeds, temperatures can reach
trillions of degrees Fahrenheit and exciting new particles are created and set free. It's a lot
like how things were just after the Big Bang, at the very beginning of the universe!

Scientists think something called the
HIGGS FIELD popped into existence just after the Big Bang.
This is what gives MASS to matter particles like me. Without mass, the
atoms that make ALL THE MATTER in the universe—including you—wouldn't
be able to form. And that would make the universe a pretty dull place!

There was one special particle that scientists were desperate to find—
a mysterious particle called the HIGGS BOSON, which is the particle
that proves the Higgs field exists—and it was finally
spotted inside the Large Hadron Collider!

A MYSTERIOUS UNIVERSE

We've almost reached the end of our mind-blowing tour, and you might think you've seen it all . . .

all the particles that make EVERYTHING that exists—and don't forget the photons that let us see all this stuff! But every star, every planet, and everything else we can see adds up to LESS THAN 5 percent of the universe.

The rest of the universe is MISSING!

IT'S A MYSTERY

When scientists looked at how stars were moving around our MILKY WAY GALAXY, they found that there wasn't enough STUFF to make all the gravity that was holding the galaxy together. This means there has to be another INVISIBLE type of matter, which they call DARK MATTER! Dark matter makes up more than a QUARTER of the universe, but scientists have no idea what it actually is.

Dark matter doesn't emit or reflect light. Because this makes it invisible, it's pretty hard to detect! Some scientists think dark matter might even be made of a completely new kind of particle called a Weakly Interacting Massive Particle, or WIMP. But they aren't sure if WIMPs even exist because they haven't spotted any yet!

BILLIONS OF YEARS FROM NOW . . .

The universe is getting BIGGER all the time, and this EXPANSION of the universe is speeding up! But why? Scientists call the mysterious force that is S-T-R-E-T-C-H-I-N-G the universe DARK ENERGY. While dark energy makes up 70 percent of the universe, scientists don't actually know what it is! If dark energy keeps getting stronger, then billions of years from now it might even tear the universe apart! Or if dark energy starts getting weaker, the universe will start shrinking. The whole universe might eventually shrink all the way down to a tiny speck, a billion times smaller than me . . .

What a way to go! Or maybe it might just be the start of a brand-new universe . . .

INDEX

GLOSSARY

absolute zero: the lowest possible temperature; the coldest it can possibly get—brrr!

atom: what every living thing and object is made of, from a grain of sand to a person to the sun

Big Bang: when, in less than a millionth of a second, the universe turned from a tiny speck into a vast space measuring billions of miles

black hole: what is left behind after a very massive star explodes

dark matter: an invisible and unknown type of matter that makes up more than a quarter of the universe

electromagnetic radiation: a form of energy that travels in waves; it includes visible light and X-rays

electron: a particle with a negative electrical charge that whizzes around the nucleus of an atom

gas: a substance with no fixed size or shape; its atoms are spread out and move around at high speeds

gravity: a force that pulls things together

helium: one of the first two atoms, along with hydrogen, in existence

hydrogen: one of the first two atoms in existence

liquid: "wet stuff," where the atoms are touching but can slide over one another

mass: the amount of matter or "stuff" a thing has in it

Milky Way: the name of the galaxy that planet Earth is part of

neutrino: a "ghost" particle that weighs almost nothing, travels super fast, and is hard to detect

neutron: a particle in the nucleus of an atom that has no electrical charge

nuclear fission: when an atom's nucleus is split, releasing a lot of energy

nuclear fusion: when a nucleus fuses with another nucleus to make a new atom, releasing a lot of energy, even more than nuclear fission

nucleus: the center of an atom

particle: an extremely tiny piece of matter

photon: a particle of light that can act like a wave and travels extremely fast

proton: a particle with a positive electrical charge in the nucleus of an atom

quark: an elementary particle, which is a particle so small that it cannot be divided into anything smaller; it makes up protons and neutrons

radioactivity: when particles break away from the nucleus of an unstable atom and radiation is released

solid: "hard stuff" with fixed shape and size; its atoms are neatly arranged and packed tightly together

star: a giant ball of gas that produces light and heat (the sun is our planet's closest star)

supernova: the explosion of a star

universe: everything that exists: billions of galaxies, trillions of stars, and countless planets

ACKNOWLEDGMENTS

The author would like to thank the following authors, scientists, and science communicators for helping me to understand more about the world of quantum physics: Jim Al-Khalili, Sean Carroll, Marcus Chown, Andrew Cohen, Brian Cox, Christopher Galfard, Brian Clegg, Brian Greene, John Gribbin, Michio Kaku, and Carlo Rovelli, as well as the authors of countless articles in *New Scientist* magazine.

 • First US edition 2024 • Library of Congress Catalog Card Number pending • ISBN 978-1-5362-3762-7 • This book was typeset in Futura. The illustrations were created digitally. Candlewick Press, 99 Dover Street, Somerville, Massachusetts 02144 • www.candlewick.com Printed in Shenzhen, Guangdong, China
24 25 26 27 28 29 CCP 10 9 8 7 6 5 4 3 2 1

I hope you've enjoyed your trip through the quantum universe. Don't forget to keep exploring!